MANCHAC SWAMP

John Kemp

Julia Sims

MANCHAC SWAMP

LOUISIANA'S UNDISCOVERED WILDERNESS

PHOTOGRAPHS BY
JULIA SIMS

INTRODUCTION BY JOHN RANDOLPH KEMP

LOUISIANA STATE UNIVERSITY PRESS
Baton Rouge and London

05 04 03 02 01 00 99 98 97 96   5 4 3 2 1

Designer: Amanda McDonald Key

Typeface: Optima

Printer and binder: Sung In Printing

Sims, Julia, 1942–

 Manchac Swamp : Louisiana's undiscovered wilderness / photographs
by Julia Sims ; introduction by John Randolph Kemp.

 p. cm.

 Includes index.

 ISBN 0-8071-2021-9 (alk. paper)

 1. Natural history—Louisiana—Manchac Swamp. 2. Nature
photography—Louisiana—Manchac Swamp. 3. Landscape photography—
Louisiana—Manchac Swamp. I. Title.

QH105.L8S55 1996

508.763'32—dc20

                                    96-13365

                                    CIP

The images in this book appear as photographed. They have not been computer al-
tered or enhanced. In addition, the wildlife photographs were taken in the wild and
not in controlled settings or captivity.

CONTENTS

To my husband, Joe Arthur, for the thousands of unselfish hours
spent with me and for me, and to my daughter, Scotty, and my
son, William, for sharing with me the land I love so

And in memory of Billy—I miss you

—Julia Sims

To Betty and Virginia, and to the people of Manchac

—John Randolph Kemp

ACKNOWLEDGMENTS

JULIA SIMS

I would like to thank the hundreds of wonderful people who helped me along the way to the completion of my book by supplying me needed information, granting me access to their private land and/or private hunting and trapping leases, or sharing with me their favorite hidden spots in the swamp. Unfortunately I cannot name them all here. For those I overlook, please realize that you are just as important to me as the individuals listed below: Virgina Rakocy; Rocky Rakocy; Charley, Jacky, and Billy Bates; J. C. Balhut; Eddie and Wayne Brescher; Donald Clark; Mark and Wanda Cortez; Warren Coco; Poncho Duhe; Edna Maye and Lawrence Duhe; Larry and Karen Dunnington; John, Carol, and Jay Dahmer; Trey Harris; Norman Danos; Jamie Richard; Mike Fannaly; Louis Barbier; Jerry and Myra Fabacher; Dennis Guy; Wayne Glasscock; Keith Hemsteter; Dago Kraft; Teddy Kraft; Latimore Smith; Mike Kliebert; Vincent Licata; Wallace and John Poole; Erick and Marie Lightell; Brad McFadden; Earl Chatellier; the Manchac bridgetenders; Beryl and Mike Robertson; Charley Sheffield; Carl and Jeff

Schneider; Hugo Succow; Bob Witte; Jerry Wagner; Kathy and Sparkey Welles; Butch and Lyle Wells; Dr. Bob Hastings; Hayden and Debbie Reno and Hayden Jr.; T. J. Denniger; Mike Hultz; Buster Hagg; Paulette Poche; Michael Polite; Stanley Ryan; Huey Husser; Enid Sears; Jamie Burns; and Richard Martin. Also the following government agencies and organizations that provided assistance: Louisiana Department of Wildlife and Fisheries; the Natural Heritage Program; Joyce Wildlife Management Area; Manchac Wildlife Management Area; U.S. Fish and Wildlife Services. And finally, I would like to express my special thanks to the staff of Louisiana State University Press, especially Amanda McDonald Key, designer, and Gerry Anders, copy editor, for their time, effort, and enthusiasm.

JOHN RANDOLPH KEMP

To Julia and Joe Arthur Sims for their patience and enthusiasm in helping me adjust to the swamp, and to Gerry Anders and the staff at LSU Press for their encouragement and enthusiasm for the project.

MANCHAC SWAMP

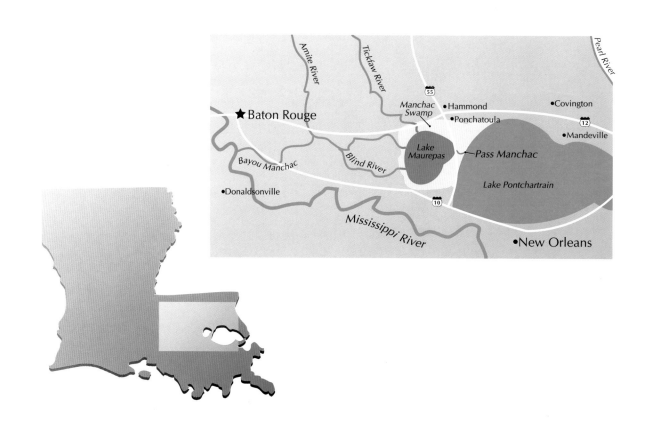

INTRODUCTION

Manchac Swamp: The Place and Its People

"Wilderness, or wildness, is a mystique," once wrote famed landscape photographer Ansel Adams. "As the fisherman depends upon the rivers, lakes and seas, and the farmer upon the land for his existence, so does mankind in general depend upon the beauty of the world for spiritual and emotional existence."

For centuries, poets and artists have explored their souls through nature. During the nineteenth century, artists such as New Jersey–born Joseph Rusling Meeker were enchanted by the dramatic sunsets and the warm, ethereal haze of foggy morning light in Louisiana's swamplands. The intense golden blush of a sunrise cutting through the low-hanging mist and thick cypress stands gave life to paintings and rhyme to sonnets. To borrow from Pat Conroy's best-selling novel *The Prince of Tides*, it is "a place where butterflies and angels are born."

Today, artists and photographers continue to search for personal expression in Louisiana's swamps, the state's only remaining wilderness areas. C. C. Lockwood has gained national attention for his striking wildlife photographs taken in the vast Atchafalaya Swamp of south central Louisiana. Over the last decade, another photographer has quietly compiled a rich portrait of a less-known Louisiana wilderness, Manchac Swamp. Julia Sims, one of only a few women professional wildlife photographers in the United States, has found expression and peace among the trappers, snakes, alligators, and hundreds of species of birds and flowers that inhabit this mysterious-sounding place with deep roots in Louisiana's past.

It is all the more mysterious because, at least to some extent, it lies hidden in plain sight. The elevated, twin-span Interstate 55 between the Louisiana towns of Ponchatoula and LaPlace crosses over a large section of the swamp, which surrounds Lake Maurepas and forms an hourglass-shaped barrier between Maurepas and its larger companion, Lake Pontchartrain. Here southbound motorists weary of Mississippi's endless loblolly pine forests and rolling clay hills get their first dramatic glimpse of south Louisiana's vast, grassy coastal prairie, which stretches from the Pearl River and Mississippi Gulf Coast to the Sabine River and Texas.

Aerial view of Manchac Swamp looking north

At the heart of Manchac Swamp, the interstate arches over Pass Manchac, a history-steeped waterway that links Lake Maurepas with Lake Pontchartrain.

Europeans first encountered the pass in 1699 when Pierre Le Moyne, sieur d'Iberville, and his brother Jean Baptiste Le Moyne, sieur de Bienville (who later founded New Orleans), explored and colonized Louisiana for France. Iberville, ever the diplomat, named Lake Pontchartrain in honor of Louis XIV's minister of marine, Louis Phélypeaux, compte de Pontchartrain, and Lake Maurepas in honor of the compte's son and successor, Jerome Phélypeaux de Maurepas. The word *manchac* first appeared in French reports in 1699 and on colonial maps in 1732. Most accounts suggest that it derives from the French *manche*, meaning "pass" or "strait," and the Mobilian or Choctaw *imashaka*, for "back way" or "rear entrance." From the many shell middens found throughout the swamp and from accounts by colonial explorers, archaeologists know that Native Americans such as the Tangipahoans hunted and fished in Manchac for centuries prior to the arrival of Europeans and well into the eighteenth century. As late as the 1860s, Choctaws, who had migrated into southeast Louisiana a hundred years earlier, had a settlement where Pass Manchac enters Lake Pontchartrain.

Pass Manchac was once an international border. During the eighteenth and early nineteenth centuries, when colonial Louisiana and the Gulf Coast bounced back and forth among France, Spain, Great Britain, and finally the United States, the pass formed part of the boundary between Louisiana and colonial West Florida, which stretched from Baton Rouge to Pensacola. During the Civil War, Manchac was an outpost for Union troops from Michigan, who feasted on roasted alligator tail while enduring the "fetid bayous. . . . musquitos, moccasin snakes," and "death-laden air of these horrible places."

Today, Pass Manchac has the less glamorous role of separating Tangipahoa and St. John the Baptist Parishes. Places such as Galva, Ruddock, and Frenier, once bustling whistle-stops along the Illinois Central Gulf Rail Road, are now little more than names on a map or exits along the interstate. Only the small Manchac community at the juncture of Pass Manchac and Lake Maurepas continues to thrive, home to a handful of trappers and commercial fishermen and the site of numerous weekend camps as well as several fish markets and a popular restaurant.

Some travelers hurry along Interstate 55, eager to put the swamp behind them. Others let their imaginations wander through the cypresses, willows, tupelo gums, and grass prairies, or slow down to take in a sunset of almost Wagnerian visual drama and colors to humble even the greatest painter. To the east, a full moon rising from the swamp throws a broad yellow path across the shadowy water. To the west, Lake Maurepas' electric blue-green surface shimmers as the sun drops below the horizon. The afterglow radiates in a cobalt-blue sky while wisps of gray clouds witness the spectacle. In minutes the sky darkens as approaching night hammers the last light into a thin, burning crimson line across the horizon.

The lyrical and transcendent beauty of nature is everywhere—in the sunset silhouetting the abandoned Manchac lighthouse, in the delicate irises and lilies struggling for survival on the tangled swamp floor, and in the chevron-winged egret preening her long, wispy white plumes with the grace of a ballerina's pirouette. Even in a spring thunderstorm, the swamp is iridescent against the heavy flannel-gray sky, towering black thunderheads, and veils of rain that sweep across the watery prairie. "The South is all for nature," wrote the French poet Charles Baudelaire. "For there nature is so beautiful and bright that nothing is left for man to desire, and he can find nothing more beautiful to invent than what he sees. There art belongs to the open air." He was describing southern Europe but could just as easily have been writing about the swamps of south Louisiana.

Unlike the pine forests a few miles to the north, the swamp has pronounced seasons. The dark greens of the oppressively hot summers are transformed by autumn. Cypresses turn russet, swamp maples and gums blaze bright red. Winter brings starkness; leaves fall away and the swamp stands desolate in brown and gray. Then comes spring with all its splendor and life. The swamp in springtime is a grand aviary with bald eagles and great blue herons nesting, stick-legged egrets stalking prey in slow motion, red-tailed hawks gliding on warm breezes, and treetops filled with the discordant songs of a thousand birds. Tender leaves cover the trees, and the swamp floor is filled with a thick field of purple irises and swamp lilies. Each season has its personality and singular beauty.

"I don't know what it is, I just love it," says Sims. "I get lost, but I mean that emotionally. I feel absolutely right. I especially love early mornings when there is a light fog. It is so still and silent. Every sound is individual and so clear. They are comforting. It's like being above the tree line in another world. You don't get that feeling on a bayou, on a river. You just get it back there. It's healing."

But danger also lurks in the dark waters beneath the soft green carpets of floating duckweed and the fallen trees whose rotting branches sway above the water's surface like large bony fingers. "I'm terrified of snakes," Sims admits, grimacing as if touched by a cold wind. "I'm afraid of alligators. If you're not afraid of a ten-foot alligator sitting on her eggs, something is wrong with you."

She remembers one afternoon when she sat in her camouflaged blind photographing a white heron rookery. She took off her hip boots to get comfortable. Her feet, clad in white socks, dangled just above the water. Then came the blood-curdling roar of two nearby alligators eyeing the rookery and a good meal. "If you've ever heard an alligator bellow, you'll never forget it. The ground literally shakes." As the gators closed in, Sims looked down to see the white socks, which could easily have been mistaken for tasty young herons. "I couldn't move fast enough. I sat there the rest of the time on my feet, Indian style."

She knows the swamp better now. "I try to use good judgment," she says simply, then adds: "But my biggest fear is people." To get a good photo of the great horned owl in its nest, she will spend the night deep in the swamp where no one ever goes except local trappers. But if the nest is on a waterway traveled by strangers, forget it. "No question! People are my greatest fear."

Like some of the swamp creatures she photographs, Sims herself is a member of a rare breed—female wildlife photographers. "It's a wild land out there, and I like that. But I'm not sure how many ladies would do

Donald Clark completing fifty-five-foot scaffolding for Julia Sims near great blue heron rookery

this. I'm not trying to prove anything. You have to love it to do it, and it's hard. It's physically hard carrying all that stuff back in the swamp." The "stuff" includes the heavy steel scaffolding she uses to photograph nests as much as seventy feet up in the trees. This is where the men come in. The scaffolding is transported by airboat to the nesting sites by Sims's trapper friend Donald Clark and her husband, Joe Arthur Sims. Several trips are needed to get it all back there. The two men assemble the platform and then leave Sims behind with her Nikons.

When Sims is after those remarkable nighttime shots of owls entering their nests,

Joe Arthur drops her off just before dark and picks her up at first light the next morning. She sits alone in the scaffolding all night, waiting for a quick glimpse of an approaching owl against a moonlit sky. When there is no moon, she shines a dim light

Joe Arthur Sims departs after bringing Julia Sims to a blind in Manchac's "Prairie."

on the nest to reveal any activity taking place. Often, the sounds made by the baby owls alert her to the arrival of the adult. As the owl descends, Sims trips the camera's shutter release and the electronic flash fires. The owls seem oblivious to the sudden bursts of light. "After all," Sims points out, "they see lightning all the time."

As an alternative to a night on the scaffolding, Sims sets up a device that shoots a pencil-thin beam of infrared light across the nest to a reflector. When the owl crosses the invisible beam, it triggers the shutter and flash. Sims picks up her camera the next morning.

Despite her airboat, cameras, lights, and scaffolding, Sims tries not to disturb the natural setting. "You are disturbing! There's no question. Your presence is always making a disturbance. But I will go to any degree to make that disturbance the least I can create. That's why we build our blinds in stages." Birds and other animals, she observes, "are like we are. Some are shy, and some will tolerate anything."

With degrees in secondary education and social work, Sims did not start out to become a professional photographer or to photo-document the Manchac Swamp. She and her husband simply enjoyed being out there. Photography came later. Sims's interest in the outdoors began while Joe Arthur was in the army and stationed in Germany. "We took up hiking in the mountains, and that opened up a whole new world to me. When we got back to Louisiana, we couldn't do that. So we took up canoeing. I enjoyed that, but it didn't give us the same feeling as being up in the mountains."

Then a friend took them deep into the Manchac Swamp in his airboat. "I had lived in Louisiana all my life, and I had never been that far back in a swamp." The next day the Simses bought an airboat.

Sims's fascination with Louisiana's wetlands began when she was a child growing up in Baton Rouge, where she was born on February 17, 1942. Her family made frequent automobile trips along Airline Highway to New Orleans. "I remember hanging out the car window as we drove through Lutcher and seeing all that beautiful swamp. I can remember thinking, 'What's back there?' There was just that wall. To think, now I'm back there. Maybe even then there was something there that drew me."

At first, photography was an excuse to spend time in the swamp: "I couldn't go out there and not do anything." Then, gradually, the camera made Sims a participant in the natural drama. After taking a beginner's photography course at Newcomb College in New Orleans, she signed up for wildlife photography workshops around the country, learning from some of the best in the business. By the mid-1980s she had a contract with a top New York stock-photo house. Her work has also appeared in *National Geographic* and an impressive list of other publications and galleries.

Although most of Sims's wildlife photography is done in Manchac, she also has worked in the Honey Island, Atchafalaya, and Houma Swamps and along the barrier islands off the Louisiana coast. "But there's no need for me to go to those other swamps. The Manchac Swamp is my backyard. An alligator is an alligator. Plus, I have good contacts in Manchac." Those contacts are the nutria trappers and alligator hunters who live in the swamp or along its outer ridges. "I get along with some pretty rough people. Rough not in a bad way, but they've been trappers all their lives, their fathers and grandfathers were trappers."

When Sims first saw these shadowy figures skimming in their fast boats across the misty swamp, she knew they would be crucial to her work. They know the swamp better than anyone. Getting to know *them*, though, was not easy. "They didn't want to have anything to do with me. They thought here's this lawyer's wife. But in time, they saw me out there before daybreak when it was twenty degrees. They saw me out there before daybreak when mosquitoes were everywhere. They saw me out there when it was ninety degrees. I was fighting the same elements they were fighting. We love the same thing."

The trappers now compete with one another in searching out interesting or rare wildlife for Sims to photograph. In return, she gives them photographs of the animals. "Their camps and trailers are wall-to-wall photographs. That's what they want. They're a neat breed. You have people who are streetwise. These people are swamp-wise." In the past, some trappers shot everything in sight. The egrets and herons that now fill photographs on hunting-camp walls were once little more than target practice on a lazy afternoon. "They don't do that any more. I've never asked them not to. They just don't." But Sims cautions would-be wildlife photographers not to head into the swamp without determining who holds leases to the land. "They'd shoot you. They will shoot you!"

Despite that cautionary note, Sims speaks of the people she has come to know in the swamp as genuine folk heroes. "They have had an influence on me. I appreciate the hard work they do. I appreciate anybody who works at what they love to do. They love it with a passion. That's why they are not depressed people. Joe Arthur says whenever I come back from being with them, I'm always so upbeat. He's says I look like hell, but I'm upbeat. They're always looking forward to something."

They are also vanishing—as endangered in their way as any rare species in a changing environment. The swamp-dweller in his boat, earning his living by every wile of hunting, trapping, and fishing, is a classic figure of Louisiana folklore. But such people were never as numerous as legend paints them, and today they are a dwindling few. "This is really the last generation," says Sims. "Their children won't be doing it."

The best way to understand the richness of Manchac Swamp is to know its people. Here are some of them.

JAMES "PONCHO" DUHE

"Poncho" Duhe was born in Reserve, Louisiana, in 1936 and speaks with a strong Cajun accent. Poncho—a nickname tagged to him in childhood—is tall with broad shoulders, a ruddy complexion, blue eyes, thinning red hair, and callused hands strong enough to crush oyster shells. He is friendly, at times gentle, but always dead serious about his work. People in the swamp speak with guarded respect about Poncho. They talk about the time the airplane-style propeller on his airboat jammed. When he tried to free the blade, it kicked over, striking him across the back three times and pinning him against a tree. The blade cut deep into his back, broke ribs, collapsed one lung, and severely damaged his spleen. He wrapped the deep gashes with his shirt and walked three miles through the swamp to get help. He drank two

James "Poncho" Duhe poles a pirogue to check crawfish traps on his swamp lease.

glasses of whiskey straight and went to the hospital. A week later, he was back trapping.

Like his father, Ambrose "Tatoon" Duhe, Poncho has spent most of his life in the swamp. "My old man used to do it, all his life, but he got too old. He stayed back here until he was eighty years old. He didn't want to keep up with it, so I took it over." Tatoon died at the age of eighty-six.

Poncho does his trapping and hunting on nine thousand acres of thick swampland leased from a lumber company. He works his lease, which stretches along the southeastern shore of Lake Maurepas, from a fishing camp his father built many years ago. Located on the Reserve Canal not far from where the canal empties into Lake Maurepas, the weathered wood-frame camp,

Poncho Duhe dining on catfish courtbouillon under warning signs in his camp kitchen

named "Tatoon's Hunting Club," is filled alligator skulls and mounted ducks, raccoons, and deer heads—trophies of two generations of hunting in the swamp. But Poncho's bedroom walls are now covered with Sims's photographs.

Like others who make their living in the swamp, Poncho follows the "seasons"— the word refers less to the calendar than to the natural and ever-various cycles of life in the swamp. "Everybody axed me if I get lonely or if it gets boring. It never gets boring. I do different t'ings at different times. I fish during the summertime and the springtime, crawfish. I do the alligator eggs in mid-July. I get a dollar each for them. I sell them to alligator farms as far away as Alexandria, Louisiana. Then after that I usually have a crop of young alligators that I turn loose. And after that I go into the alligator season in September. That lasts another month. October, I go to squirrel and rabbit huntin'. In winter comes the deer huntin'. Then I do my trappin' in December, January, and February. I don't do the same t'ing like I had a job to get up at the same time." Poncho once had regular jobs—on oil rigs, in sugarcane fields, and doing automobile body work— but they took too much time away from trapping and hunting. "This is all I do right now."

Poncho Duhe releasing two-year-old alligator into swamp

One September morning, the second day of alligator season in south Louisiana, Poncho and his crew were in their airboats deep in the swamp checking Poncho's alligator lines. He had caught eleven alligators the day before; he had state permits for at least thirty-four more.

Poncho's boat glided through the wilderness along trails of water as black as

Louisiana crude, crossing mud flats, sunken stumps, and cypress logs. A grove of palmettoes swayed lazily in a rare September breeze like cardboard handfans on a hot Sunday morning in church. The steamy air was only slightly thinner than swamp water and smelled of mud and rotting vegetation. The square-nosed boat pushed muddy waves over upcroppings of dark cypress knees as it cut through islands of floating water hyacinths, lime-green duckweed, and sawgrass. Raised-headed cottonmouth moccasins, sleek green frogs, and young alligators fled the deafening roar of the airboat's engine. Poncho, sitting high in the pilot's seat, maneuvered through tricky turns with the calm confidence of someone born to the wilderness. He pointed out signs of alligators. By the paths swimming gators cut through the duckweed and water grass, he can tell how large they were and how long ago they passed.

Poncho's alligator lines are nothing more than heavy cord tied to a branch at one end with a large baited hook at the other. The bait, usually chicken wings or thighs, hangs two or three feet above the water to keep smaller alligators from hooking themselves. As Poncho eased his boat among the trees, some lines hung as he had left them, the bait untouched. He nodded; this was not unusual. Some hooks dangled empty: owls had taken the bait. Still others were pulled taut into the black water. This usually meant a snared gator. Small ones hooked in the mouth were thrown back for another time. Large ones were fair game.

Toward the end of the run, Poncho came upon a line stretched tight. He pulled, and the weight was like a submerged stump. The gator would not budge. Poncho's friend and cousin Donald Cambre lent a hand. The huge, reluctant creature rose slowly. As its head broke the water's surface, the gator began to thrash wildly, rolling over and over, its whiplike tail slashing mud in all directions. Wide, powerful jaws opened and hissed a threatening defiance at the two men until three shots from Poncho's rifle ended the five-minute drama. The dead gator measured ten feet nine inches in length.

One late Sunday afternoon in early February, Charles Kraft was in the small wooden skinning shed at the end of a cluttered path behind his house, off a narrow road west of Ponchatoula and fifteen minutes from Pass Manchac. A lifelong trapper and fisher-

man in Manchac Swamp, "Dago"—his nickname to everyone—worked in the skinning shed almost every afternoon during nutria season.

A single fluorescent light illuminated the dark, dank one-room structure. Steel-jawed traps hung from one wall. A dried beaver pelt was nailed next to the door. A flirtatious calendar girl stared out from another wall above drying nutria skins. On two sides of the shed, row after row of drying nutria, mink, and otter pelts hung to dry. Below one rack of hides, hundreds of dried pelts lay stacked like firewood.

At a small, brown-stained table in the center of the room, Dago cleaned his day's trappings. His razor-sharp knife gliding over the pelts' pink inner surface, he cut away meat and unwanted tissue with the deftness of a

Charles "Dago" Kraft at his skinning shed

surgeon. At the back of the shed an ancient, rusty clothes dryer clanked along in metallic rhythm, drying fresh skins. When each pelt was clean, Dago stretched it over a cypress drying board, nailed it in place, hung it to dry, and reached into the machine for the next one.

Dago, with tangled black hair and skin tanned as dark as a dried pelt, looked exactly the part of one of the last remaining trappers in Manchac Swamp. He was talkative but shy, rarely making eye contact with those around him. As he nailed skins to the drying board, streams of sweat ran down his brown, whisker-stubbled chin like a heavy rain across burned swamp grass. "About forty years ago," he said, "I stayed out there in that swamp about fifteen years. I run away from school and I stayed in the swamp. I got as far as the sixth grade. Dey kept me after school one day and I jumped out the window, went down to the swamp, and never come back out of there."

Trapping has changed considerably over the years, Dago said. "I started trappin' when I was twelve or fourteen, and dey didn't have no nutria in those days. Didn't have nothin' but mink and muskrat. Dey ain't got a muskrat in that swamp now. Dey just disappeared. Lots of coons, nutria—and minks are just startin' to come back. Da prettiest fur dey got is a beaver, and dey won't buy it. Dey never would buy beaver down here." Mink pelts that once sold for $22 to $25 now fetch $4 to $8. Mink farms have knocked the bottom from under mink trappers. The price for nutria hides is much lower—so low that in 1993 Kraft did not bother to set his traps. "It was the first time in forty years I didn't trap. It wasn't worth nothin'. Dey wouldn't buy 'em."

As if conscious of belonging to a disappearing way of life, Kraft noted that he preferred to run the traplines on his lease in an old-fashioned pirogue, rather than use one of the now-popular motorized Go-Devils or airboats: "I don't like dem airboats." He added that his son, Charles, is not a trapper, but a crabber in Pointe a la Hache, near the mouth of the Mississippi River.

As Dago talked, Luther Morehouse walked into the shed. Morehouse, who lives in Slidell, has been a fur buyer for over thirty years. He was there to buy Dago's pelts, but like all good storytelling Cajuns, he was prepared to reminisce: "I remember back in the days when buyers came from all over the country to buy pelts. Dey ain't no more nutria like dey used to have. You used to come over here and you'd see thirty-seven thousand of 'em. It'd take 'em four days to count and grade 'em. One man shot dice out there and lost all his money, thousands of dollars. One roll, double or nothin'. That was about twenty-five years ago. All the big dealers who use to be in the business are all dead. Yeah, we had some nutria there one time. Dey might come back."

After Luther's departure, Dago, too, spoke of the long view. "I'd rather trap than anything. That's the best thing I did ever like to do in my life. I just love it back there. Been in it all my life. But it done changed ten times since I've been in it. It's wide open now. I've seen deer, you couldn't shoot from here to that door right here without hitting one, it was so thick. You'd have to cut your way through. Deer, hogs, everything. It's wide open now, everyt'ing died. I don't know what killed it. Dey say salt water killed it, salt water ain't killed it. I don't know. I feel sick back there now, da way it looks. It looks bad." Perhaps his mood reflected thoughts of what he might learn the following day at the doctor's office. The next day came and his fears were reality: he had cancer and faced a long series of operations. A few months later Dago was back on the lake crabbing. But a year after that Sunday afternoon in the skinning shed, the cancer finally triumphed, and the old-time Manchac trappers were fewer by one.

ERICK AND JUSTILLIA MARIE PONVILLE LIGHTELL

Erick and Justillia Marie Lightell live at the end of a long shell road in the little settlement of Frenier Beach. Their house is a camp raised high off the ground on creosote

Marie and Erick Lightell

pilings in the traditional style of the south Louisiana marsh. Less than a hundred feet from their front door, waves from Lake Pontchartrain slap against a breakwater of broken concrete slabs. Jet airliners interrupt the silence as they work their flight patterns around nearby New Orleans International Airport.

Erick and Marie have lived in Manchac Swamp for as long as they can remember. Erick was born in St. Bernard Parish, just south of New Orleans, but at the age of four went to live with his grandfather, Oscar Lightell, at Frenier Beach on property owned by the Guste family of New Orleans. Oscar worked for the Gustes and made extra money selling catfish, shrimp, and trout and trapping mink, coon, and otter.

Marie was born in LaPlace. Her family moved to Manchac when she was a very young child. "My brother and daddy use to trap along Highway 51." Her strong rhythmic Cajun accent snapped out the words in short bursts like slapping mosquitoes on a warm summer night. "We had a palmetto house, and it had cardboard for floorin'. When my mama went into labor, dey called Doctor Gross. He crossed the canal. My daddy went and get him. He said, 'Oh! It's goin' to be cold in here for dat baby and your wife, she gunna catch pneumonia.' So after the baby was born, he took her and put her in a box, my sister in a box, near the stove. The box was catchin' on fire. My mama said, 'Where's my baby?' Doctor Gross said, 'I wrapped her up and trow her in a box.' And daddy said, 'Yeah, but that box is on fire.' My mama used to tell us that story all the time." Marie's ninety-year-old mother speaks only French. When she goes to the hospital or doctor's office, Marie accompanies her as a translator.

Marie's father built the palmetto house when she was about five or six. It had three bedrooms and a kitchen. Palmetto fronds overlapping on a pole frame formed the roof and sides—a style of construction adapted by French colonists from the Indians. "It didn't rain in it, and it was nice and warm." The family lived there until the early 1950s when the highway department moved them out to make room for a new Highway 51. With free lumber given by a friend, Marie's father built another house nearby. Twenty years later, they were in the way once more. The interstate was coming through and highway officials "told us to move again, so we moved back by my sister's house in LaPlace." After the Lightells' son was born, the Guste family gave them permission to build a camp on the Frenier Beach property. What began as a weekend camp eventually became a home.

The Lightells are as much a part of the swamp's rhythm as the changing tides. Erick sells catfish, lizards, snakes, and frogs and runs crab traps in Lake Pontchartrain. Marie makes and sells stuffed crabs and flounders. Like many others in Manchac, the Lightells tend to look away shyly when talking with strangers, rarely making eye contact.

The couple's large living room, with windows overlooking the lake and nearby fishing camps, is filled with photographs of their son Erick, known by friends and family as "Poule d'eau" (pronounced "pool-doo" in Louisiana, and a common nickname for children in French-speaking parts of the state, the term names a small waterfowl, the American coot). The bright, cheerful photographs were a melancholy contrast to the framed obituaries that hung across the room. "I don't know how it happened," Marie said, her voice painfully balanced between despair and attempted good spirits. "He was by himself. I don't know if he fell overboard or what. He was crabbing. It was on a Good Friday." In one corner stood a vase filled with brown, wilted flowers—the bouquet of red roses Poule d'eau gave his mother a few weeks before he drowned. "You see, I still got them. They all dried up, but I told him I was never goin' to trow them away."

Despite their loss, the Lightells still love the swamp: its beauty, and the freedom it brings to their lives. "It's quiet," says Erick. "I think about a lot of stuff. I worked before on different jobs and I just didn't like it. Here, you are your own boss. Nobody's on your back all the time. You wanna go, you go. You don't wanna go, you don't." To Erick the swamp is at its best in the early morning. "Everything is quiet, everything is starting to wake up. You see more animals moving around early in them morning." Winter mornings, "especially when there's a frost on the ground," are the most peaceful times to him. Marie prefers summertime, when the trees are in full green.

Like everyone who knows Manchac Swamp, the Lightells have noticed great changes taking place. "Every year things change more and more," Erick says. He describes those changes one by one. Erosion is the biggest problem: "The lake taking up everything, eating up the land. After a while the washout will be all the way out here. No protection, just getting bigger and bigger. We also catch more she-crabs coming from the Gulf. I've never seen that before. The lake is getting more salty than before."

The middle-aged Chicago couple could not resist the sign hanging in front of Virginia Rakocy's little white cinder-block seafood market at Manchac. Driving along Interstate 55, they could see her sign below, advertising everything from alligator to coon meat. When the couple walked in, they quickly were aware that this was no ordinary

Virginia May Rakocy sorting soft-shell crabs

fish market. Tags in the display cooler identified wild pig, coon, nutria, muskrat, alligator, and turtle, along with catfish and soft-shell crabs. Five alligator skulls rested atop the cooler, their dark bony eye sockets and fearsome teeth confronting anyone entering the screen door. The couple bought five pounds of alligator meat and in a few minutes were back in their white Cadillac heading home to Chicago.

Virginia, who runs the market with her fisherman son Andrew "Rocky" Rakocy, is an elegant woman with penetrating eyes and a lilting laugh. Half the people in the Manchac area call her "the bait lady," but somehow only the last word seems to fit. Born the year World War I broke out in Europe, she has lived in Manchac her entire life except for a brief time during World War II when she worked in Monterey, California. Over the years, she has fished, worked as a waitress in a Manchac restaurant, and during the late 1940s and early 1950s, served as postmistress at Manchac's tiny Akers Post Office (named for Will Akers, a longtime railroad telegrapher at the Manchac bridge). Three times a day, she met the trains to pick up or send out the mail. The trains also took on fresh fish for New Orleans and other towns and cities along the track.

"You are just so free here," says Virginia of her long life in Manchac. "I guess I just love the changin' seasons. It keeps me so occupied. You just look forward to the alligator season, the deer huntin' time, the trappin' time, the crabbin' and fishin' time. There's just always somethin' to keep you lookin' forward to."

Virginia's late husband, Andy, drove a school bus up to Ponchatoula for over thirty years. "He had fifty-five children at times. After the second road came through, they took people's land and many of them moved to town. A few young people

Rocky Rakocy pulling up crab pot

stayed." Shortly after Andy started driving the bus, Virginia opened a small seafood market under a shed alongside the highway and in front of the house she and her family lived in for over forty years. "I started selling crabs, a little bait, and all that right under that shed." She pointed outside to the small shed, where local fishermen and trappers still congregate to socialize and talk about their catch, prices, or any other topic of the day. "I get three or four bushels of crabs a day now, when I use to get forty bushels a day."

Virginia's family, the Saltzmans, came to Manchac from Blind River, in Livingston Parish, on April 10, 1896. She has spent many years compiling notes on the history of Manchac and its families. She reads from her notebook: "They crossed Lake Maurepas to Manchac

and bought 365 acres at 25 cents an acre. The Saltzmans learned how to fish here. At Blind River they were farmers and mink trappers; they also cut cypress to make roof shakes for houses." She has notes on Manchac's early families, the Barbiers, Succows, Renos, DeGruyses, Windeckers, Straders, Cortezes, and Guichets—the latter being one of the few African-American families to settle in Manchac. She also had stories about the German families at Frenier—Groetes, Windeckers, Slussers—who grew cabbage on their small farms and from it made sauerkraut that they shipped to New Orleans, Chicago, and St. Louis. The farms are all gone now. Most were destroyed by the devastating 1915 hurricane.

Virginia was too young to remember that storm, which took many lives and wrecked almost every building in Manchac. But she does remember Hurricane Betsy in 1965. "The only thing I don't like and really don't like is hurricanes." She put one hand to the side of her head to emphasize the story about to come. When Hurricane Betsy hit in 1965, Virginia, Rocky, Andy, and Andy's grandfather huddled in the house, listening to a battery-operated radio. "We heard the announcer say, 'The eye of the hurricane is here!' I didn't realize what the eye of a hurricane was. It was about midnight or later, I seen this big bright light coming across the lake on the railroad bridge. I said, now that's the eye of a hurricane. So we got our raincoats and hats, and I made grandpa put on his rain coat. I said, 'This *must* be the eye of the hurricane.' Then I heard a roar and sure enough I knew it was the eye. It turned out to be a freight train." Her head rocked back as she laughed at her own innocence.

Virginia talked about Manchac and its beauty before the interstate blocked her view of Lake Maurepas and its shoreline. "This interstate wasn't here." She pointed an accusatory finger out the front door to the raised concrete roadway. "Out on that point there was some beautiful cypress trees and the moss was hanging. They would be green—just beautiful. You could feel the cool in the evening. I would go out there and just watch. That old canal wasn't there....There's nothin' beautiful on that lakeshore any more. Not like it was. It just don't look the same."

DONALD CLARK

"There's a word that describes Donald," Sims says, but after struggling to find that one word, she settles for several: "He literally becomes part of the environment, and his eyesight is unbelievable." Clark catches birds and snakes with his bare hands. The creatures seem oblivious to his presence. "One day I was with him and his wife out in the Prairie in a marshy area. All of a sudden Donald ran his boat up on the ground, jumped over Ruth, and just took off running. Next thing you know, he has a mallard

Donald Clark on nutria hunt

duck under his arm. He ran around a little more and then he had two mallard ducks under his arm. He can just approach these animals and they don't leave."

Clark, a retiring and shy man with a mop of dark brown hair, makes his living following the seasons in the swamp. He started working in Manchac at the age of eight with his stepfather, Robert Kliebert, who owned a turtle farm in Hammond. After finishing high school, Donald "graduated from school to the swamp." He hunts nutria and catches catfish, crickets (for bait), lizards, and snakes by day and frogs at night. When he is not hunting, fishing, or frogging, he often can be found building scaffolding to provide Sims a closer look at the nest of a horned owl or red-shouldered hawk. Over the years, he has given her another set of eyes in the swamp.

Clark is one of the few trappers who work the Manchac Swamp on foot. He owns boats, but when he nutria hunts, he takes off and walks five or six miles. He shoots nutria rather than trapping them, skins them on the spot, and leaves the flesh for other animals. He also walks the railroad track through the swamp, catching lizards and snakes. He has been bitten twice by venomous cottonmouth moccasins. His remedy is one every scout learns—cut the bite and bleed it. But he does his best to avoid cottonmouths. "You can smell them, they stink. You can smell them when you are around them."

Like others who spend their lives in Manchac Swamp, Clark is fiercely independent. "It's somethin' I like. You don't have to listen to nobody." He once worked as a scaffold builder for Shell Oil. In 1985

Hand-catching animals such as this diamond-backed water snake is a knack of Donald Clark's.

the company sent him to Arizona, but he quickly returned to Louisiana and Manchac. He uses only enough words to make his point: "No swamp. Nothin' to do but work. When they ain't workin', they drink."

Donald Clark hefts seventy-pound loggerhead turtle

Although Clark does not talk much to strangers, he breaks through his reticence when the subject is the swamp and the beauty he sees out there—especially in the morning light with the "sun coming up and a misty fog on the ground." He often picks wildflowers by the root and transplants them in his yard. Clark refuses to take money for helping Sims build scaffolding or spot wildlife. Instead, he wants photographs of the creatures he long took for granted. "The real thing is always prettier. But with a picture, you can always remember it when you can't go back." Sims believes her photography has changed Clark's attitudes toward the swamp and its wildlife. He once told her that before he met her, he was not too concerned about what he shot out there. Now he has books about birds and often phones Sims to talk about the different species in his bird feeder.

MICHAEL HENRY FANNALY

"I love it. You can get back there and it's real quiet. You're by yourself and you're part of nature. I see things in my life that Julia would love to have on film. You just see things other people will never see. I can leave my truck and in five minutes see more things than any person can, paying twenty dollars to go on one of those swamp tours."

Michael Henry Fannaly, born in 1953 of Irish and German descent, is tall with a thick athletic build and wavy ginger hair. His blue eyes and every inch of his clean-shaven, ruddy face enjoy a smile. A lifetime of pulling shrimp nets and crab traps and paddling pirogues has given him thick fingers and strong hands. His life as a commercial fisherman in Manchac and Lake Pontchartrain began when he was eleven years old. "I use to put the crab traps right up in front of the pass [Manchac] and get a few crabs and sell them to Middendorf's Restaurant. I got thirty-five cents a dozen. They'd bring them up and sell them for fifty cents a dozen. Back then, thirty-five cents was a lot of money." After high school, Fannaly had ideas of becoming a marine biologist. He spent two years studying botany at Southeastern Louisiana University in nearby Hammond, but then got married and headed back to the swamp.

When Fannaly is not crabbing, he is shrimping, fishing, trapping alligators and nutria, or catching frogs and crawfish on his nine-thousand-acre lease, which stretches along Lake Maurepas from Pass Manchac south almost to the Reserve Canal. He has held the lease for more than a dozen years. Before that, leases were rare among the trappers and fishermen. "It was open land. Fishermen and trappers had unwritten agreements as to individual territory. You just honored where he went. If he had a run, you just stayed off it."

Fannaly has seen many changes in Manchac since he was an eleven-year-old

Mike Fannaly heading out at daybreak to fish Lake Pontchartrain at the "hole" near the mouth of Pass Manchac and the lighthouse

with a few crab traps. Not only is the swamp's very nature changing, but trappers and fishermen are having a more difficult time making a living. Fannaly outlines the problem with the ease of a broker discussing the stock market: "The product I catch is worth more, but there's not as much of it. Ten years ago, you could go and just about walk across the lake on crab traps. You couldn't find a place to put them because there were so many. Last fall, when I crossed from the pass to the south end of the causeway [Lake Pontchartrain Causeway], I ran across one line. People have thinned out that much in the last few years." Fannaly also believes that crabbing in Lake Pontchartrain has been seriously hurt by overharvesting and by seafood brokers from northern states buying up everything that is caught.

"When we first started crabbing, you couldn't sell a gumbo crab [small crab]. The only thing you could sell was a number one crab. Anything else, we would throw them back. When these dealers came down, they put a price on what they call factory crabs. You can't afford to throw them back. You're talking thirty-two dollars a bushel. That's a lot of money. These crabs are going to Bayou

Mike Fannaly pulling in shrimp trawl fitted with sea-turtle excluder device

La Batre, Alabama, and the picking plants, and that's the crabmeat that you buy."

The fur business also is not what it was. Manchac Swamp was once filled with muskrat, otter, and mink. A few remain, but most are gone. The three-cornered grass that muskrats once dined on was destroyed by salt water and nutria. Even the formerly high-rolling nutria business has declined dramatically since its peak in the 1970s. "Fur sales used to be a big deal down here. Buyers came from New York, all over. They bought whatever I had. It's been five years since we had one of those. Use to be a good deal for everybody involved. Now, there's just very few people trappin'. The hardest thing is finding somebody to buy them."

Fannaly believes the day may come when he can no longer make a living crabbing or trapping in Manchac. But whatever happens, he will not give up the swamp where he has spent most of his life. "This is all I've ever done. If I couldn't do it full time, I guess I would spend most of what I made going down there duck huntin', deer huntin'. I'd be down there one way or another."

Dennis Guy and his wife, Denise, live near French Settlement at the end of a long, dusty dirt road bordered on both sides by swamp. Their house is on the Chinquapin

Dennis Guy trimming end of cypress log

Canal, which leads to Bayou Chene Blanc and eventually Lake Maurepas. Guy's yard is filled with machine parts, a large metal-roofed shed covering a sawmill, and cypress "sinker" logs scoured from nearby bayou and lake bottoms. The massive tree trunks scattered about the yard resemble felled columns from some toppled Athenian temple transported to a Louisiana swamp.

The dark, crusty logs, which have lain on the water bottoms for almost a century, generally run three to four feet in diameter. Many are more than a thousand years old. Against the side of the Guys' two-story, alpine-style home, which Dennis built himself totally from sinker cypress, leans a cross section of a cypress log almost five feet in diameter. The tree was a sapling in the time of Christ. Guy built his house entirely with planks from this and other ancient logs found nearby. Walls and floors throughout the house are made from this exquisite wood with the warm color of buttered honey. Individual floorboards measure as much as twenty-six inches wide.

Guy is in his early fifties and has the build of a man who wrestles water-soaked logs out of the mud. His face is leathery brown and his graying hair is an unruly mass. When he smiles, the crinkles around his green eyes break into a worn sunburst.

Guy, who works by himself, has been milling sinker cypress logs

The top of a freshly milled sinker cypress log makes a warmly glowing walkway for Dennis Guy's granddaughter, Mandy Spitchly.

for over a decade. Finding them and wrestling them up from water bottoms is hard work. First he scouts likely spots—along the edge of Lake Maurepas, the nearby bayous where logging was heaviest, and train crossings where logs where hoisted from the water to waiting flatcars. Standing in his boat, Guy eases along "feeling" the bottom with a pole. When he strikes something that feels like a log, he jumps overboard and dives to the bottom to test the object with his hands. "I stick my hands in the mud like a turtle." Guy burrows his wiggling hands in the mudless air to show how it is done.

Hayden Reno, wife Debbie, and son Hayden Jr. raise a sinker log from the Ruddock Canal.

To raise the sinker, Guy uses his homemade pontoon boat, a cleverly designed little craft made entirely from found parts. The pontoons are joined together by a superstructure of steel pipes. Pulleys and cables hang from the metal frame. At one end of the main cable sits a large winch seasoned by rust and motor oil. Steel logging tongs hang at the other end. Guy lowers the tongs to grip the log, then hoists it until it rests directly between the pontoons, where he secures it with heavy steel cables. "I spent as much as ten days getting a log up once," he says matter-of-factly. "I fought it until I finally got it."

Once the sinker is in place, Guy tows the pontoon rig back to his mill. He uses his backhoe to drag the log from the water. When the wood is dry enough for milling, he muscles the log into position for the saw with the help of cables, winches, and pry bars. He uses a bandsaw rather than a circular saw because the bandsaw creates less waste. The blade moves lengthwise down the log, slicing off wide boards like a sharp knife cutting through a slab of cured bacon. Guy mills only cypress, which he sells by word of mouth to builders, cabinetmakers, and anyone else who enjoys working in the material. "There's no prettier wood than this," he says firmly.

Hayden Reno would agree. One balmy June morning Hayden, his wife Debbie, and their son, Hayden, Jr., were aboard their homemade pontoon rig in Manchac Swamp pulling a large sinker log from the muddy bottom of Black Bayou. The rig creaked and rocked in the shade of an eight-foot-thick hollow cypress on the nearby bank. The tree's hollow core saved it from the lumberman's axe a century ago. Yet the tree still lives.

The Reno name has been known in the Manchac area since those early logging days, and Hayden Sr. has lived in Manchac Swamp all his life. For more than eighteen of his thirty-seven years he made his living following the "seasons" in the swamp—fishing, frogging, trapping alligators, and pulling sinker cypress logs from the bottom. Although he is now the full-time caretaker at Southeastern Louisiana University's Turtle Cove Environmental Research Station at Pass Manchac, he still hauls his rusting pontoon rig out into the swamp and bayous to pull logs.

"I used to pull ten thousand feet a week out of these canals," Hayden said while adjusting a cable around the water-soaked log dangling between the pontoons. "I got log sinkers around here I got hid. I got logs bigger than that." He nodded at the three-foot-thick log in his cable rigging. "That log went all the way across the canal. I wouldn't leave it in shallow water, so I hid it. I just got it in my head where I leave logs. I used to get in the canal and just walk. I used to do it every day. I used to come pull logs all day by myself and spend all day from sunup to dark."

Falling cypress prices, aging equipment, and "cold winters" finally persuaded Reno to look for more dependable work, but he still gets out in the swamp as often as possible. "It's in my blood," he says, glancing at his son playing on the huge, water-blackened cypress log. "Somethin' about this swamp and water. I just love it. I like in the spring when it's still cool. I love it in the winter. It's all dead and you can see things. You can find all kinds of stuff from loggin' days. I should have been back here a hundred years ago."

LOUIS HENRY BARBIER

From an airplane overflying Manchac Swamp, the effects of a century of cypress logging are painfully visible. Within sight of the New Orleans skyline to the southeast, vast grassy prairies soak in coffee-black water where a thick cypress forest once stood. What remains today are thousands of dark stumps rotting in the mire, third-growth cypresses struggling for survival, thousands of felled trees graying in the hot sun, and narrow logging canals cutting across the watery landscape like long-festering wounds.

Aerial view of Cecil's Canal in Manchac Swamp shows the radial lines of old logging pullboat run.

To satisfy south Louisiana's and the nation's appetite for cypress, logging companies almost leveled the entire Manchac area between the late 1890s and 1956, when the last log was cut for the mills. They crisscrossed the landscape digging canals such as Main Canal, Ruddock Canal, and Galva Canal to move their steam-powered pullboats deeper and deeper into the swamp. From each canal, small feeder ditches radiate off in every direction like spokes in a wagon wheel. From the air, these watery radiants glisten like silver starbursts in the late afternoon sun.

Cypress logging was a major industry in Louisiana, especially in Tangipahoa and St. John the Baptist Parishes. Manchac prospered, and boom towns such as Frenier, Ruddock, and Strader popped up along the railroad line that had opened the swamp and its vast forests to the world (the first highway, a dirt road, did not come along until 1926). By 1910, Frenier had almost two hundred residents, a small Catholic church, and by 1914, a school. Ruddock's population in 1915 was over seven hundred. Workers filled the towns and lumber mills. When they were not cutting trees or milling lumber, they fished, trapped, and gathered Spanish moss, which in those days was widely used in stuffing mattresses and padding upholstery.

But in September of 1915, life in Manchac changed forever. The great hurricane of 1915 roared through. After it passed, Ruddock and Frenier no longer existed and more than 275 people were dead, mostly in south Louisiana (in Frenier alone, 25 people were killed when the railroad depot, in which they had sought refuge, collapsed).

Louis Henry Barbier at age ninety-nine

The once-thriving communities were never rebuilt, and the swamp long ago reclaimed the few surviving house pilings.

Louis Henry Barbier of Ponchatoula was in New Orleans when the 1915 storm hit, but he remembers the hurricane that hit Manchac and southeastern Louisiana on September 21, 1909, as if it were only yesterday. "My mother, my uncle George, and my sister and my brother were there when the storm hit. The water was washin' in the front door. We thought we were gone. All the camps down there gone. On the big lake [Pontchartrain], that had big timber, big cypress timber, it was just like a break boat went along there. I'll bet that storm blowed every bit a hundred and twenty miles or thirty miles an hour. You could hear it come across the South Pass when it hit our place—just like a freight train." The storm, which packed winds up to 125 miles per hour, claimed more than 350 lives, again mostly in south Louisiana.

Born in Madisonville, Louisiana, on May 17, 1896, Barbier remembers the thick cypress swamp well. The son of a French-speaking Swiss immigrant, he grew up on Jones Island in Manchac Swamp. Just before the turn of the century, his father purchased seventeen acres on the island. There he built a house and raised a family. The little homestead had a smokehouse, vegetable gardens, and fruit and pecan trees. Barbier's father made his living trapping, fishing, and hunting alligators. "I remember he killed some sixty-odd alligators in one night. He took the hides and left the carcasses in the swamp." Hides then sold for twenty-five cents a linear foot (today a large gator fetches more than forty dollars per foot). "They had all kinds of stuff down there. I came out one day with sixteen minks, twenty-two coon hides. We had to skin 'em back there in the swamps. They were too heavy to carry out. Them days I was a big man. I could pick up half a deer and walk out the swamps with them." Barbier's grandmother operated a small stall in the New Orleans French Market selling game and fish her husband caught in Manchac. "We use to paddle along Pass Manchac right at the edge of the swamp and kill us a couple of squirrels while goin' home. Now you can't see a squirrel or a rabbit or nothin' else. They all killed out. The young generation ruined the world. That's what they done." His voice grew angry as his hands dug deep into the armrest of the overstuffed chair while pulling his frail body up closer to the edge of the seat. "They kill everything they see. When the poules d'eau and the ducks would come down there, the pass would be black with them."

Barbier, whose small frame house in Ponchatoula is filled with faded family photographs, remembered when the logging companies practically clear-cut Manchac. In fact, he worked for the companies. "I was about seventeen or eighteen when they done all that. They just pulled boats in there. I worked on a pullboat, cuttin' timber. I would cut the tree around." Ringing the trees cut off their sap flow and killed them. They were then left standing for as long as a year before being logged and floated to the mills. During that time the wood dried, losing weight and thus becoming easier to handle. The technique of ringing cypresses was learned by the early French settlers, probably from the Indians. "We got fifteen cents a tree, that's all we got," Barbier recalls. "Them big trees, sometimes took you an hour to go around them."

Life in Manchac was hard and medical care scarce. Barbier's mother died of pneumonia when he was fifteen. "We had to wait a day before we could get a doctor." His father sent him to live with an aunt in New Orleans. After returning from service in World War I, Barbier and his bride, Allie, from Osyka, Mississippi, moved to Manchac, where he took a job at Edward Schlieder's elaborate Turtle Cove fishing camp on Pass Manchac. Schlieder was an executive with Salmen Brick and Lumber, one of several companies that held vast timber leases in the swamp. Barbier later worked as a lightkeeper's assistant at the Manchac lighthouse, an important navigational landmark then located on dry land where the pass entered Lake Pontchartrain. Today the lighthouse, which Barbier swears is haunted, stands abandoned and in ruins several hundred yards out in the lake.

Barbier began as the assistant keeper and later became head keeper, a job he held until the Coast Guard abandoned the lighthouse in 1958. He recalls stormy nights and rowing a small boat through treacherous seas to service seven beacon lights in Lake Pontchartrain and four in Lake Maurepas. He remembers the steamboat *Alexander Stuart* and the schooner *Malvena Anderson* and other steamers and schooners that hauled freight to and from New Orleans through Pass Manchac. He remembers twin-engine towboats "pulling a mile of timber at a time through the pass." Cypress logs were chained together in huge "rafts" that were pulled through the Pass and then across Lake Pontchartrain to the mills. "Sometime those logs would get heavy, so they would cut them loose. They would sink to the bottom. The bottom of the pass down there is filled with big timber." He described the cemetery that still can be seen "near North Pass and the big oak tree," where sixteen members of the Barbier, Saltzman, Reno, and Jones families are buried. "I got an uncle, two brothers, and a grandmother buried down there." Virginia Rakocy's four-month-old son, who died of pneumonia in 1934, also is buried there. An elaborately carved wooden plaque once marked his grave, but it was destroyed during Hurricane Betsy. A simple wooden cross now throws a gray shadow across the burial site.

Sadness rises in Barbier's voice when he talks about the changes he has seen in the swamp over nearly a century. "When I drive across the Manchac bridge, I shake my head sometimes...nothing but a lake. Ain't no more timber in there...cleaned it all out. I don't even try to go down there anymore."

A DYING SWAMP

Louis Henry Barbier, Poncho Duhe, Virginia May Rakocy, Michael Fannaly, Hayden Reno, Erick and Marie Lightell, and others who have lived their lives in and around the Manchac Swamp know that the swamp is slowly dying. Fannaly describes the Manchac of the late 1950s and early 1960s: "When I was a kid, you could go off the side of South Pass and you could get lost there. It was actually that thick—myrtle bushes, palmettoes, the trees and cypress were alive. They weren't big, but everything was alive. They used to have plenty of deer and ducks. They used to have so many ducks, you'd go in some places, you couldn't hear yourself talk. It's all more or less open now. The salt water, I think, more or less killed it. Just after Hurricane Betsy in 1965, that's when things really started dying off."

Latimore Smith taking core sample from a virgin tidewater red cypress to determine its age. The trees are now rare in the United States. Many of those surviving in the Manchac Swamp area are more than five hundred years old.

Scientists and state agencies are working on several fronts to save Manchac Swamp, which, according to Louisiana Department of Wildlife and Fisheries plant ecologist Latimore Smith, contains some of the oldest tidewater red cypresses in the country. Between 1975 and 1977 the state created the Manchac Wildlife Management Area with the purchase of more than 8,000 acres of swamp and marsh, including the once-broad, grassy plains called the "Prairie." In 1982 the Joyce Foundation of Chicago donated 13,569 acres of swampland to the Louisiana Department of Wildlife and Fisheries. The department then leased another 2,040 acres from landowners to form the Joyce Wildlife Management Area. In addition, biologists at the Turtle Cove Environmental Research Station have initiated a program to plant cypress seedlings, hoping to rebuild the forests. They have planted thousands. Many have survived, but most have been eaten by nutria.

The station's director, Robert Hastings, is not optimistic that Manchac can be saved. Hastings, a wiry man with close-cropped graying hair and beard, claims that natural and human-engendered forces are slowly killing the swamp. Clear-cut logging, which continued as late as the 1950s, is not the only culprit. Hastings enumerates other factors: natural land subsidence; rising sea levels caused by long-term global warming; the digging of logging and highway canals; the Mississippi River levee system, which prevents natural sediment deposits in the swamp; and the depredations of nutria, a South American rodent that spread explosively in the Louisiana wild after being released by accident from a breeding farm in the 1930s.

The now-abandoned Manchac Lighthouse once stood on dry land.

Lake Pontchartrain's salinity is a complicating—and complicated—factor. It increased somewhat after the completion in 1963 of the Mississippi River–Gulf Outlet shipping canal, which connects New Orleans and the Gulf of Mexico, but Hastings suspects that salt water entering the lakes from the Gulf during hurricanes causes far more damage than long-term trends. In 1985 Hurricane Juan brought a six-foot tidal surge into the lake. Everything in Manchac flooded. When the water receded, salt was left behind in the soil. High salinity in the lake may be good for shrimp and the seafood industry, Hastings says, but it is deadly for cypress.

Scientists generally agree that land subsidence, the lack of new sediment deposits from the Mississippi River, and the intrusion of Lake Pontchartrain's naturally brackish waters are harming the swamp's cypress shoreline. Not all scientists, however, accept Hastings' salinity theories. In a 1985 article, estuarine ecologist Walter Sikora, then at Louisiana State University, and oceanographer Bjorn Kjerfve of the University of South Carolina pointed toward natural land subsidence as the main culprit. As the land slowly subsides, they wrote, more and more water from the lake enters deeper into the swamp, killing fresh-water vegetation. Their study also found that salinity increased only slightly in eastern Lake Pontchartrain after the Gulf Outlet opened, and hardly at all near Manchac to the west. As for hurricanes, Sikora and Kjerfve suggest that any temporary increase in salinity caused by seawater incursion is more than offset by the heavy rainfall that accompanies hurricanes, flushing the lakes with fresh water from area rivers.

Whatever the cause or causes, the cypress swamps around the rim of Lake Pontchartrain have eroded at the rate of 15 to 23 feet a year since 1970. By comparison, the Manchac area lost only about 300 feet of shoreline between 1897 and 1952. As late as 1953, the Prairie was just that, a broad grassland. In the 1970s, it was 70 percent water. By 1990, it was 90 percent water.

Professor Hastings believes Manchac's slow death is inevitable. "It cannot be stopped. It can, however, be slowed down. We have to remember that the earth is a very changing environment. It is not stable....Manchac is disappearing along with much of the rest of the Louisiana coast. The estimated rate for all Louisiana is about thirty-five square miles per year. The distance from Lake Pontchartrain to Lake Maurepas by Pass Manchac is seven miles. The loss of the Prairie is definitely imminent. Only twenty-five or thirty yards of land separate it from the lake. If we lose the Prairie, that means two of those seven miles are lost." If Hastings' dire prediction comes true, Pontchartrain and Maurepas eventually will become one large body of water and Manchac will be little more than a memory on old maps and in Julia Sims's photographs.

Photography, Ansel Adams once wrote, has an obligation "to help us see more clearly and more deeply, and to reveal to others the grandeurs and potentials of the one and only world which we inhabit." Manchac is Julia Sims's world—an undiscovered one for most of us—and through her photographs we can see its fragile yet timeless grandeur.

SPRING

Great egrets in breeding plumage marking their nest in spring. The green coloring around the eyes is most intense during courtship but begins to fade when the eggs are being laid.

Great egret, preening, with her young. Great egrets are
steadfast guards of their nests.

Viceroy butterfly gathering pollen from swamp rose

Spider lilies

Great egret feeding freshly caught fish to young

Young great egret coaxing mother

Spring bouquet of morning glories, cypress vine, and tie vine along Manchac highway

Manchac cypresses in spring greenery

Male and female cattle egrets marking nest site, early spring. Ornithologists believe that the cattle egret arrived in the Western Hemisphere from its native Africa sometime in the early twentieth century. They suspect that a flock of the birds may have been caught in a storm off the coast of Africa and blown to South America. Cattle egrets arrived in Louisiana in the 1950s by way of the Caribbean islands and Florida.

(center)
Cattle egrets mating

(above)
Cattle egret in rookery, early morning

(overleaf)
Early morning in cypress swamp

Great blue heron with chick
demanding to be fed

Little blue heron showing off her
breeding plumage

Male and female roseate spoonbills, related to
ibises and storks, and fairly rare in Louisiana

Tri-colored heron, once known as the "Louisiana heron," in breeding plumage, gathering
sticks for a nest

Snowy egret protecting her nest. Also called "golden slipper" because its feet appear to have been dipped in gold, the snowy egret was slaughtered for its plumage in the 1920s. The birds are now protected by law.

Yellow-crowned night herons exchanging watch over their nest

Wing-net shrimp boat coming in at sunrise after a night's work

Skeleton of old cypress tree

Female (left) and male anhingas in breeding plumage and mating dance. The birds, native to Louisiana, migrate to South America during the winter. Anhingas are also known as "water turkeys" and as "snakebirds"—the latter because they swim with only their head and neck above water.

"You first." Two six-week-old barred owlets glance at each other as their mother, from another tree nearby, coaxes them to fly. The young birds both took their first flight soon afterward.

Screech owl bringing frog to chicks in nest. This image was made using an infrared-beam device that triggers camera and flash when the beam is broken—in this case, by the arriving owl.

Barred owlets, four weeks old

(left)
Water lilies and American lotuses

(above)
Water lilies

Sunset, Lake Maurepas

Fishermen in Pass Manchac, early morning

Raccoon with baby

Common gallinule nesting with chicks

Red-shouldered hawk feeding green snake to chicks. All three chicks were later killed by crows, mortal enemies of the hawks.

(overleaf)
White ibises returning to roost at sunset

Nutria stripping bark from tree. Nutria, natives of South America, escaped from a breeding farm into the Louisiana swamps in the 1930s. They quickly proliferated and today constitute a major destructive force in wetland environments.

Otter eating freshly caught fish

Scene in Four Mile Marsh

Cypresses, Spanish moss, and a watery carpet of duckweed

Red maple, mid-February; the burst of color is a signal of spring in south Louisiana.

SUMMER

Morning glories along Manchac highway

American lotus bloom with bee gathering pollen

Cypress vine

Great egret feeding among water hyacinths

Rare "blue" lizard; the coloration results from a genetic mutation.

Alligator with egret

Small alligator under water

Female alligator protecting nest

Dick Wall collecting and marking alligator eggs while watching
for mother gator

Rare albino alligator

Black-necked stilt fishing in the "Prairie," part of the state-owned Manchac Wildlife Management Area

Abandoned lighthouse on Lake Pontchartrain at Pass Manchac

Least bittern, an extremely shy bird native to Louisiana. Rarely seen but often heard in Manchac, the least bittern makes a *kok-kok-kok* cry distinct from the American bittern's *oonk-a-lunk* call.

Abandoned pirogue. Originally, these shallow-draft canoes were one-piece dugouts made by the Indian method of carving them from cypress logs. Later, flat-bottomed board pirogues became the norm, but cypress remained the wood of choice.

Teddy Kraft casting net in Pass Manchac. He uses the catch to bait his catfish lines.

Camp on Lake Maurepas. Shoreline erosion left the camp, once on dry land, totally surrounded by water. A month after this photograph was taken, a summer storm destroyed the structure.

Rat snake sunning

"Blue" bullfrog on lily pad. As with the blue lizard, the rare coloration results from a mutant gene.

Tree frog

Mike Fannaly frogging

Abandoned trapper's camp

Purple gallinule, "marsh hen," using lily pads as a fishing platform

White-tailed deer fawn

Prothonotary warbler, "swamp canary," feeding worm to young

Red-bellied woodpecker with beetle for her young

Male killdeer feigning injury to draw intruders away from its nest

Young pileated woodpeckers peeking from nest. The lower bird is a male, larger and more brightly colored than his sister.

Red-eared turtle with alligator nearby

The still backwaters of Manchac Swamp create a mirror world reflecting cypresses and a young snowy egret feeding in the early morning light.

FALL

Cypresses at the entry of the Amite River into Lake Maurepas

Wing-net shrimpers before sunrise in Pass Manchac. Shrimp migrating from Lake Pontchartrain to Lake Maurepas travel through the pass by night. Moving at or near the surface, they fall prey to the wing-netters. (Shrimping is not allowed on Lake Maurepas itself.)

Cypresses in morning mist

Barn swallows arriving in Manchac on southern migration

Setting sun on cypresses, Lake Maurepas

Sunset on Lake Maurepas

Eddie Bresher and Jacky "Big Head" Bates placing duck decoys in Manchac Swamp

Warren Coco, president of the Baton Rouge-based Go-Devil Manufacturers, Inc., in a duck blind off Mississippi Bayou

Alligator going for baited hook. Largely because of poaching, alligators were vanishing from Louisiana thirty years ago. Today improved wildlife-management procedures have increased the gator population to the point where tens of thousands are legally taken each year by professional trappers.

Moonlight on Lily Bayou

Hunter returning from morning outing in Manchac Swamp

(overleaf)
Early morning mist in Manchac

Bobcat prowling. In Louisiana, bobcats are found mostly in pine uplands and heavily wooded swamps. Relatively numerous in the state and trapped on a limited basis for their fur, the animals are listed as a "Table 2" endangered species nationally.

Hunter on morning outing in Manchac Swamp

Sunset on Blind River and Lake Maurepas

Camp on Blind River near Lake Maurepas

White ibises feeding in the "Prairie"

Female anhinga drying wings in early morning fog

Autumn field of fourchettes (bur marigolds, or "sticktights") in marsh

Cardinal flower in morning dew

Mark Cortez, in his boat *Swamp Rat*, shrimping "the hole" on Lake Pontchartrain near the mouth of Pass Manchac

Muskrat mound in Four Mile Marsh in the Joyce Wildlife Management Area. Once found by the millions in south Louisiana, muskrats have all but vanished from the swamps. A principal factor in their decline is habitat depredation by nutria.

WINTER

American coots or poules d'eau (pronounced "pool-doo" in Louisiana) making take-off run on water

Ice on cypress stumps along the south shore of Lake Maurepas, February 1996

Lake Maurepas. These two cypress trees were once part of the swamp habitat but now stand in open water because of the lake's encroachment.

Abandoned pushboat, Lake Maurepas

Great horned owl egg with protruding "egg tooth"

Great horned owl chick about ten days old with baby nutria brought by mother for baby's food

Great horned owl and chick eating mouse

Charley "Loggerhead" Bates going crabbing

Sunset, North Pass looking out over Lake Maurepas

Southern bald eagle in cypress tree

Southern bald eagle bringing four-pound catfish to her chicks in cypress-tree nest. Once almost extinct in the lower forty-eight states, the bald eagle is making a comeback in Louisiana and throughout the country. Wildlife experts recently counted more than a hundred bald eagle nests in Louisiana. In the 1970s only twenty were known.

Winter in the cypress swamp

Joe Arthur Sims picking "oyster" mushrooms, a Manchac delicacy

(overleaf)
Foggy morning in Manchac

Raccoon settling into hollow of tree for the day

"Manchac's Elsa" on a frosty morning in the swamp
(Julia Sims's yellow Labrador almost always
accompanies her on her expeditions)

Otter eating on log

Male wood duck in his brightest plumage

Nutria guarding nest

131

Warren Coco arriving at hunting camp on the western edge of Manchac Swamp

Trapper Mike Kliebert savors the aroma of a batch of alligator sauce piquante.

Bald eagle silhouetted at sunrise

Moonrise at North Pass

Beaver family resting on den

Gray fox close to her den. Native and common to Louisiana woodlands,
gray foxes are trapped commercially in winter for their fur. Up to eight hundred Louisiana
gray fox pelts are sent to Canadian fur processors annually.

Six-point buck in winter's high water

Dawn on Buzzard Bayou in Manchac

Sunrise near Amite River

INDEX